Don't Misunderstand Me

I Want Your Vote!

Political Talk Edition

A humorous look at the mismatch between what politicians say and what they're really thinking.

Merrilee Kimble
Jason Myers

Don't Misunderstand Me
I Want Your Vote!
Political Talk Edition
By Merrilee Kimble & Jason Myers

Copyright © 2008 by CleverLivingOnline.com, LLC

Published by CleverLivingOnline.com, LLC

For information write, to books@dontmisunderstandme.com

Drawings by Merrilee Kimble

Mk©

ISBN: 978-0-615-24981-0

First Printing

Introduction

Welcome to the third installment of the runaway-hit book series *Don't Misunderstand Me*. If you're looking for a humor-filled and, dare we say, sarcastic or perhaps brutally honest view of what politicians say versus what they actually mean . . . sit back, relax, and read on.

At some point in history, weren't elections held only once a year? Now it seems there is an explosion in the number of politicians and political offices, and elections take place every couple of months. Whether the political stage is local, state, or national, the candidates parade around with the same recycled messages election after election.

With the increase in the number of elections comes the staggering number of political speeches from candidates who are stumping for your vote. Over and over again, we hear the same phrases and promises. How is it possible that so many candidates speak, at the core, very similar messages?

Could it be that politicians secretly share something in common in their DNA? Perhaps they share a secret book of phrases. Once a phrase is spoken and deemed "politically correct," it becomes a sacred part of a secret book. Or could it be that they simply never tire of hearing their own voices? If only the electing public could say that they never tire of hearing their voices and their messages.

Whether it's attacking opponents, attacking the opposition party in its entirety, making promises that are seemingly impossible to fulfill, or telling a few whoppers about their own backgrounds, politicians just can't be stopped.

A quick look through the editorial pages provides endless descriptions of politicians and their messages: nonsense, infuriating, misleading, flip-flopping, insensitive, fear-mongering, failing, slamming, debunking, attacking, defending, double-talking, and distorting.

The descriptions of politicians' actions are nearly as mind-numbing as the actions of the politicians themselves. It seems there is no end in sight to the routine. Politicians continue to spread their messages, and the voting public grows more and more disenfranchised with the process. So what are we to do? In our opinion, laughter is good medicine.

In some sense, it could be considered optimistic to believe that there is actually more thinking behind these favorite phrases, and we dare to hope that is the case! Even more human-like, perhaps there is a bit of political incorrectness behind all the politically correct language?

We've set out in this book to gather some of the phrases politicians like to repeat, in some form or fashion, ad nauseam. We then put on our thinking hats to determine what politicians might actually be thinking while they speak these phrases. When they say they want to save the world and cut taxes, are they really thinking "yeah right" or perhaps "when pigs fly"? No, maybe they are actually thinking "but first I must run to my phone booth and put on my super-hero outfit!" That one gets our vote.

Call it cynical. Call it negative. We just call it good clean fun and laughter. After all, why spend your life taking things seriously when you have the choice to lower the frustration threshold and just enjoy some good laughter. At this point in time, the evidence of history seems to indicate that politicians are not about to change their tunes or their messages.

After you read this book, we hope you find yourself wondering what politicians are really thinking when they speak and then replace a few moments of frustration with your own laughter.

"I believe we are on an irreversible trend toward more freedom and democracy but that could change."

- Dan Quayle

Spoken -

"Your concerns matter to me."

Meanings & Thoughts -

Although I may not remember your concerns tomorrow.

Unless, of course, I can't do anything about your concerns. Then they matter, but I can't do anything about them.

I have reserved spot number 69,837,239 on the list of concerns for your issue! I'm sure we will work on that soon. You just need to practice some patience.

Spoken -

"I will not…"

Meanings & Thoughts -

However, I could change my mind or possibly "forget" if at some point in the future I decide that "I will . . ." The most important thing is to be decisive . . . for the moment!

If my approval ratings will be helped though, I might have to reconsider.

Unless I can blame homeland security, the economy, or the opposition party. Then all bets are off.

Spoken -

"I have never…"

Meanings & Thoughts -

That I "recall." After all, as I recall it, I cannot be held responsible for things I've done if I don't recall doing them.

I do reserve the right to do so at some point in the future. After all, we're talking about the past, not the future!

My opponent certainly has, just ask him! Come on…ask him!

Spoken -

"My experience speaks for itself."

Meanings & Thoughts -

Duh!

Okay, I actually don't know the answer to your question. So maybe you can figure out if my experience answers the question. Next?

Your question bores me, and I can't stand the thought of answering you.

Spoken -

"I'm just like you."

Meanings & Thoughts -

So trust me to take care of all these political matters. You just relax and vote for me, and I'll take it from there. I've got it all under control.

Even though I really don't know much about you, I'm sure we are absolutely alike. We may have been separated at birth.

The only difference is that I want to speak for you and make decisions for you. Kind of like a spouse. Aren't we a perfect match?

Spoken -

"It's time for change."

Meanings & Thoughts -

All prior positions and statements are now deemed irrelevant, unless of course they are relevant, and then we wouldn't consider them irrelevant.

Obviously, the current plan is just not working so we are back to the drawing board.

My opponent is just stupid and unless you want a stupid person with stupid ideas representing you I'd say it's time for a change! Wouldn't you?

Spoken -

"I've fought successfully to..."

Meanings & Thoughts -

I was initially opposed, but then when I learned that several special interest groups were supporting it, I gave them many opportunities to convince me that it was the right move.

You don't know how many excessive lunches, dinners, and cocktails went into forming and passing that legislation.

I may not have proposed the legislation or had my name on it or spoken out in favor of it, but I voted for it and that makes my support critical to the passage of the legislation.

Spoken -

"There will be no more excuses."

Meanings & Thoughts -

So take that! I'm stepping up to the plate! Clearly I may have ridden the excuse train a little too long.

I'm wiping the slate clean of all prior excuses, and I am therefore no longer responsible for any excuses I made in the past!

Going forward, I will be offering explanations, not excuses! That's a BIG DIFFERENCE!

Spoken -

"I support…"

Meanings & Thoughts -

And as soon as someone does something about it, I will certainly jump on board and support that idea.

I don't plan to do anything about it myself, but I certainly support the idea.

I can't be held responsible for anything actually happening as a result of my support. Do you know what it would take to create change?

Spoken -

"I have worked on numerous efforts to…"

Meanings & Thoughts -

The fact that there have been numerous efforts and we still have the problem is really immaterial.

What is important is that we did something. Successful or not, what is most important is that we tried really hard, over and over again.

We just need to keep throwing things at the wall to see what sticks!

Spoken -

"Washington's failure to…"

Meanings & Thoughts -

Let me be clear…it's all their fault! It's not my fault.

If I were elected to office, I would change everything about Washington. Maybe even the name. What's with "DC" anyhow?

I should be hailed a hero just for having to deal with such inferior people as those in Washington!

Spoken -

"This job isn't about doing what's easy. It's about doing what's hard. It's about doing what's right."

Meanings & Thoughts -

If what's right just happens to be easy, then it's "ok" because right trumps easy every time. So as long as it was right, we can no longer call it easy.

If only it was about doing what's easy! Good grief that would be a dream job! I would want that job for sure!

Fortunately, I am an expert judge of what's right. I consider myself to be right all the time. I can't think of a time when I was wrong. I don't think it's ever happened.

Spoken -

"I'll stand up and tell you what you need to hear."

Meanings & Thoughts -

So there! Take that!

The fact that you may not like to hear what you need to hear is therefore irrelevant. I have the microphone!

I think you're very lucky to have a person like me to determine what it is that you need to hear and to then tell you. You're welcome!

Spoken -

"I fought to eliminate the tax!"

Meanings & Thoughts -

It's not my fault it didn't happen.

It was the opposition party's fault. They are the root cause of everything that goes wrong. If it were only up to our party, we would be able to do everything we need to. We just can't be expected to work together!

After all, it's not whether you win or lose, it's how you play the game…or something like that!

Spoken -

"We can't be afraid to stand up when our future is at stake."

Meanings & Thoughts -

I find that talking about issues is the most important thing we can do! Then we need to form committees to thoroughly discuss, research, and explore the options and then develop numerous possible solutions. Then we will form sub-committees to talk, research, and explore each of those options and then develop possible additional solutions. After all, our future is at stake!

However, we should never blame any of my past votes and/or decisions for any issues that arise in the future. I'm quite sure that everything was the opposition party's fault.

Spoken -

"We need to unite around a common purpose."

Meanings & Thoughts -

For example, we can start with uniting around getting me elected. I fully support that common purpose!

I prefer to support popular issues that get me lots of votes. Way more bang for the buck, if you ask me!

That means we all have to do our share. If it doesn't work, we all take the blame! If it does work, it was my leadership that made it happen!

Spoken -

"Today I want to lay out my plan."

Meanings & Thoughts -

Certain restrictions apply.

Limited time offer.

Certain taxes, costs, economic impacts, and other irrelevant calculations may have been omitted from the analysis.

Not responsible for errors and omissions.

Subject to change if no one likes it perhaps before I even step off the stage.

Spoken -

"This will be costly in the short term."

Meanings & Thoughts -

Don't think of it as your money; think of it as government money! Government money is completely different. It might not even be green.

After all, I have a lot of campaign donors I owe favors to. I'll be able to pay off all kinds of favors with this project.

I suppose you could say the entire project is costly, but that is just so negative. I think we should just look at it as costly in the short term and not focus on it being costly as an overall project! We shouldn't think beyond my term in office, that's just not reasonable.

Spoken -

"I'm motivated by the people, not special interest groups."

Meanings & Thoughts -

Though I am sensitive to the fact that special interest groups are made up of people and I am motivated by the people.

I only have meetings, dinners, cocktails, and lunches with special interest groups so I can tell them in no uncertain terms that I'm not motivated by them.

I suppose you could call any political party a special interest group but no, that's just ridiculous.

Spoken -

"I am a leader you can believe in."

Meanings & Thoughts -

Trust me! Really, what's the worst that could happen?

I care about you and your concerns and issues and all that blah, blah, blah stuff!

I like to consider myself to be a Super-Hero. I call myself "Super-Hero-Dan-The-Political-Man"! You trust and believe in Super-Heroes so you can certainly trust me.

Spoken -

"I oppose wasteful spending."

Meanings & Thoughts -

It cuts into the government pay-raise structure that I support, and I need a raise!

It keeps me from being able to help fund meaningful projects like my proposed four-year study of government spending, which would allow us to analyze everything we spent over the last decade to look for wasteful spending. My cousin's company is perfectly suited to perform this work.

However, not all wasteful spending is actually wasteful. Who is really to say what's wasteful spending? What's wasteful to you might be purposeful and meaningful to someone else. Can't we just all get along?

Sometimes we have to look the other way because wasteful spending is tied to legislation that has a great purpose. When that's the case, we can't call it wasteful!

Spoken -

"I will stand up for our country."

Meanings & Thoughts -

If our security is threatened, I'm not afraid to send troops in take care of business. Once things are safe, I'll be right there beside them, standing up for our country!

As a town commissioner, my decisions are likely to have national impact! The president may call me in to give counsel on issues of national security. I don't actually know the President or anyone in Washington, but I have a respected background and I am very important!

Spoken -

"During my first day in office, I will…"

Meanings & Thoughts -

First, I am definitely going to put my feet on the desk and then spin around in the chair until I get dizzy. That's just good clean fun!

Now, I will need some time to settle in, and then I will declare when I consider it to be my first day "in office." There is a difference between my first day "at the office" and my first day "in office." I anticipate that my first day "in office" will be about three to six months after my first day "at the office," and that is when I will really get things started.

Spoken -

"We are all in this together."

Meanings & Thoughts -

We shouldn't focus on blame or responsibility! What's important is that we all just keep supporting me!

I really need all of you to come together and let me know what we need to do because I'm stumped on this one! If it doesn't work out, it's important to note that I just did what you told me to do.

Together, we just need to vote for me!

Spoken -

"We need to restore trust."

Meanings & Thoughts -

And trust me when I say you certainly can't trust my opponent!

If we could just stop looking into everyone's background, we would stop finding so many things of concern. Then we could restore trust!

I feel that it's my role to let you know everyone you can't trust so then you will know that you can trust me!

Spoken -

"I believe…"

Meanings & Thoughts -

So there!

I don't know for sure that what I believe is actually true or accurate, but I believe it's true and accurate, and isn't that all that really matters?

It's better to believe than to not believe. If you don't believe, how would you know what to think?

Spoken -

"I am the only candidate who supports…"

Meanings & Thoughts -

Others may be saying that they support this, but I know that I'm the only candidate who really supports it!

Dibs! I called it first!

Hmm…maybe that is not such a good thing. It seemed like a good thing on paper, but now that I say it out loud, I'm not so sure. I may need to change my mind on this.

Spoken -

"I will ask the hard questions."

Meanings & Thoughts -

Even when I don't know the answers or perhaps especially when I don't know the answers!

If I don't ask the tough questions, who will? Besides, if I'm not doing the asking, then others might be asking me.

But I have no intentions of answering any hard questions! I mean, that is just not fair. I need time to prepare and consult with experts who can tell me what I think! Let's be reasonable.

Spoken -

"It is time to turn the page. It is time to write a new chapter."

Meanings & Thoughts -

Let's just let go of the mistakes of the past and move forward. Of course, I'm referring only to any mistakes that I or my party may have made. The mistakes of my opponent or any member of the opposition party are extremely relevant!

Face it we just can't fix this current mess. The best thing we can do is to forget about it, ignore it, and move forward!

Change is good! Let's all embrace change!

Spoken -

"We must do more."

Meanings & Thoughts -

That should not be confused with "we have not done enough." That's just negative.

We need to throw everything against the wall and see what sticks. It might cost more and we might not actually know what worked, but that is a small price to pay.

We've done little so far, and apparently that is not working.

Spoken -

"My commitment to you is . . ."

Meanings & Thoughts -

Unlike promises, commitments can be broken, re-evaluated, or even re-scheduled. That makes a lot more sense than promises which will get you every time!

I think being willing to make the commitment is really the most important measure of success. We shouldn't be so focused on the results unless they're good! In that event, results are all that matter!

Spoken -

"We have to work hard to get back to…"

Meanings & Thoughts -

Moving forward is a very bad thing because we don't know what's there. If we go back and repeat things, we'll know what happens in the future!

We shouldn't try new things; we should just do the same things we've done in the past until they start working again! That's the way to do things.

Spoken -

"We need aggressive action, and we need it now!"

Meanings & Thoughts -

Keeping me in office is aggressive action, and I certainly need that right now!

Somebody better do something!

Spoken -

"The last thing you need is more talk."

Meanings & Thoughts -

And, frankly, I'm just tired of talking. So if you could just go vote for me, we can wrap this up, and I can move into my office and start planning my next vacation.

There's only one person who takes credit for everything good this team does, and that's me.

It's cute that you think you deserve some credit.

Spoken -

"We don't need more rhetoric, we need action."

Meanings & Thoughts -

It's official. We have talked about it for six years, and apparently that alone didn't fix it. Go figure!

Put a cork in it. My head is going to explode if I have to hear one more conversation on this topic.

Spoken -

"I would work with leaders from both parties."

Meanings & Thoughts -

The leaders are just stupid but I'll work with them, if I must. Morons!

If things don't go according to plan, it's their fault, not mine! Let's be clear about that!

I'll just need to align them both with a common special interest group, and it'll be smooth sailing.

Spoken -

"I'll keep my word to the American people. You can trust me!"

Meanings & Thoughts -

What do you have to lose?

I find that the less you do, the less you can get in trouble for. So I'll keep my work to a minimum and you can be sure of that.

I'm the most hard-headed person ever. You can count on me not changing my word! I won't even consider what other people have to say or any circumstances at the time.

Spoken -

"If I'm elected, we're going to . . ."

Meanings & Thoughts -

P-A-R-T-Y!

Ride this office to my real ambition. I just need to pick the most controversial topics so I can get the most camera time, and I'm a shoe-in for the next office! Weeeeeee!

Tell everyone else what they should be doing and why their lack of action has prevented us from being able to do all the things we said we would.

Laugh uncontrollably at the opposition party. We won, and they lost!

Spoken -

"Leaders don't fear change!"

Meanings & Thoughts -

After all, we just tell other people what to do differently. We don't actually do anything ourselves!

We just don't like to actually make change. It's not because we are afraid of change though! It's just that it's hard and it takes a lot of work!

Spoken -

"I'll work with . . ."

Meanings & Thoughts -

I doubt they will do anything I tell them to do, but I'll work with them.

Although I can't be held responsible, unless it turns out well. After all, it was my idea!

Spoken -

"I will make my case to every American who will listen."

Meanings & Thoughts -

I like to travel around and talk: it makes me feel very important. Plus, I get to tell everyone else what they should be doing to make things happen.

My mother used to say I would talk 24 hours a day, 7 days a week, and 365 days a year if I could!

If you won't listen, then shame on you!

Spoken -

"I will try to persuade others. I will debate and learn. I will not yield when it comes to what I think is right."

Meanings & Thoughts -

After all, you can't tell others how wrong they are if you don't let them tell you what they think.

I really consider myself all-knowing, and I'm always right. My challenge is to make sure that others understand that I'm always right and they are just not!

Just give me a topic, any topic, and I can tell you how wrong you are regardless of what you say! This is how I bring people together.

Spoken -

"I would be best to lead that effort."

Meanings & Thoughts -

I'm a natural-born leader! I'll show you!

Please, oh please, oh please. I really want to lead, and I would be really good at!

This effort is a piece of cake so I want this one. Easy feather in my cap.

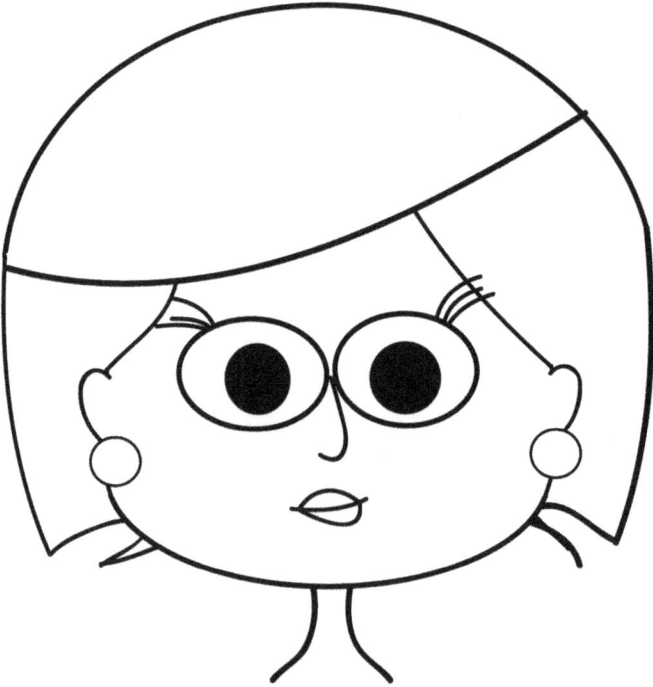

Spoken -

"No one running for this office has the kind of experience I've had!"

Meanings & Thoughts -

I have been investigated numerous times by authorities and have always been cleared of wrongdoing.

I know who to know and what you need to know to get the things done that the people with the dough want done.

Spoken -

"We just need to leave the past behind so we can focus on the future."

Meanings & Thoughts -

Let's just wipe the slate clean of any current criticisms of me and move forward. Of course, anything my opponent has done is the past we can't dismiss because I'm sure he is just going to repeat it in the future!

I do reserve the right to continue to point out any of my success in the past and use those against my opponent whenever possible.

Spoken -

"We need someone who can restore our moral leadership."

Meanings & Thoughts -

What do you have to say to that? Huh?

I think it's more important to be moral than good. I will spend my time in office spreading my moral messages.

People need me to tell them how they should think on issues. I have special powers.

Spoken -

"I think I'm the only one who can do it."

Meanings & Thoughts -

My opponent is a chuckle-head. Do you really think a chuckle-head can do it?

Some people say I have a big ego. They are insignificant little morons.

If you think otherwise, you're wrong!

Spoken -

"We have to stop worrying about the problems and thinking we can't deal with them."

Meanings & Thoughts -

There has just been too much thinking going on. We need to stop thinking!

We need to move from thinking to talking. Then in a few years we can move from talking to doing. We don't want to rush taking action though; I've got a lot on my plate right now.

Planning ahead is really over-rated. Everything will be just fine. Trust me!

Spoken -

"It's clear that will be easier said than done."

Meanings & Thoughts -

Just in case we don't get it done, let's start laying some groundwork for excuses.

Though it's really not even that easy to say so perhaps we are not giving enough credit for even saying it!

Spoken –

"My opponent represents the failed policy and fear-mongering of the past."

Meanings & Thoughts -

He's perfect if you are looking for a whiney loser. Heck, he might even be a whiney boozer!

Oh yes, I said "mongering." I learned that word on my word-a-day calendar!

Spoken -

"This is good for the country."

Meanings & Thoughts -

Hold on to your chairs, this should be fun!

The fact that I need to point this out makes me think that some of you might not think this is good for the country. What's up with that?

Spoken -

"I stand for . . ."

Meanings & Thoughts –

I would sit for it, but apparently everyone wants a person to stand!

I'm sure that very soon I will even accomplish something that will demonstrate what I stand for.

Spoken -

"I look forward to debating my opponent on that topic!"

Meanings & Thoughts -

I first need to talk to my advisors so I can find out where I stand on the issue!

I can take 'em. I know I can. Good grief, I hope this works!

Spoken -

"We need accountability."

Meanings & Thoughts -

And since this is my first election, you can't make me accountable for anything! That works well!

Which is why I'm going to tell you everything my opponent has done wrong.

Spoken -

"My opponent's record speaks for itself."

Meanings & Thoughts -

And it's going to need to because I'm not sure what his record is. I'll bet it's bad though. Yeah, it's got to be bad!

If I had a record like that, I'd skip the country and change my identity.

Spoken -

"I have a vision that will take this office to a new level."

Meanings & Thoughts -

This is my stepping stone to big things, and I plan to use it to its fullest to promote my political future.

I will use this office to gain as much media coverage as possible! Everyone will know my name.

I'll have my fingers in everyone else's business. I'll be all over every opportunity.

Spoken -

"I believe in a government that represents the citizens, not just special interest groups."

Meanings & Thoughts -

That is not to say that we should ignore special interests. I prefer to just align myself with the popular special interest groups!

However, we must keep in mind that the special interest groups are made up of citizens!

As long as I represent special interest groups composed of citizens, then I have covered the bases and am not supporting "only" special interests.

Spoken -

"We must work together to achieve our common goals."

Meanings & Thoughts -

We'll come up with a proposal and then the opposition party will come up with a proposal and then we can spend our time telling each other why the other's plan is wrong but we'll do it together.

Bipartisan is like a bipolar artisan, creative and multi-focused.

You vote for me, and I'll vote for me! Now, that's a common goal!

Spoken -

"Wasteful spending is out of control, and I plan to change that!"

Meanings & Thoughts -

And I think a good-sized pay increase will be an appropriate reward for reducing wasteful spending.

First, we will need to change the label of wasteful spending and reserve that term exclusively for spending by the opposition party.

Now, to help people understand my plan to curb wasteful spending, I will travel by private jet to Iowa, Florida, California, Illinois, and all parts in between to share it firsthand.

Spoken -

"I will fight for and protect the American worker!"

Meanings & Thoughts -

Some folks may need to lose their jobs but it will be in the name of protection.

By sending jobs overseas, we will make things better for American workers. After all, they won't have so much work to do, and they can relax more.

I'll make sure to protect the unions, because they protect the workers.

Spoken -

"The rich should pay more in taxes."

Meanings & Thoughts -

Lucky bastards, let's stick it to them!

They must be punished for their success. After all, the more you make, the more you should pay. It just makes sense.

I mean we already do but, I can look like a commoner if I declare war on the rich!

Spoken -

"I will restore your trust in our political system."

Meanings & Thoughts -

I can also leap tall buildings in a single bound!

And I believe in Santa Claus! I know he is not supposed to be real, but I think he is! The Easter Bunny is clearly made-up but not Santa Claus!

I trust it even though I don't know how it works. You should too.

Spoken -

"We must have balanced and responsible fiscal policies."

Meanings & Thoughts -

We just need to tax more, and then we can spend more. That keeps it all balanced.

I don't personally even balance my checkbook, but I'm sure someone around here knows how to do it.

I think exercise in school and after work will help people be more fiscal, right?

Spoken -

"I have spent my life fighting for Americans."

Meanings & Thoughts -

What have you done?

Some call it being a "career politician". That's just an ugly tag.

Spoken -

"I'm running to keep the American Dream alive!"

Meanings & Thoughts -

It has always been my dream to hold office so clearly that is an American Dream, and I need you to vote for me and keep it alive!

Without me, the dream will die. I'm just that good.

My American Dream is to win this political position and if I lose, clearly the American Dream dies for all!

Spoken -

"We must keep the faith!"

Meanings & Thoughts -

And I'm crossing my fingers and my toes!

If you have faith, that automatically means you are good. It's just a natural fit! You shouldn't try to fight it.

If you keep the faith, I can keep face.

Spoken -

"We must invest in the future of our children!"

Meanings & Thoughts -

Investing is such a better way to say "spending money."

Can you really say "no" to a little child? They are so cute. Let's focus on their cuteness, not the spending.

No child's future taxes left behind! Yeah that's the ticket.

Spoken -

"Sometimes we have to be able to laugh at ourselves."

Meanings & Thoughts -

And just hope that everyone is not rolling around on the floor with explosive laughter at the same time!

After all, if mistakes are made, it's important that we just laugh it off. Let's never hold grudges!

And, most importantly, we have to be able to laugh at our opponents, including voters who don't vote for us.

Spoken -

"What this country needs is my expertise."

Meanings & Thoughts -

Because I'm all that and a can of pudding!

My opponent can't come close to my experience . . . I'm smoking hot!

My spouse says so. My parents say so. I've always been called a "know it all," which is a compliment!

Spoken -

"What we need now is change."

Meanings & Thoughts -

And we should get that change rolling by electing me!

I always say, when at first things don't succeed, change, change, change!

You could say that change got us to this point of needing change . . . that's a conundrum! However, I'm sure change now will be the right change and not the wrong change.

Spoken -

"I'm not just a politician who follows the party line. We need to get out of the box with our thinking."

Meanings & Thoughts -

We've tried the same thing over and over and over and, WOW, the same results each time. Go figure!

I checked with the party beforehand, and they said it's ok to think outside the "party line" as long as I review it with them first. That's very open thinking!

It's important to weigh the views of special interest groups also. Sometimes their view is even more important than the party's.

"Those who stand for nothing fall for anything."

- Alexander Hamilton

We hope you enjoyed a ton of good laughs!

Politics and politicians can be frustrating. However, when you turn a bit of that frustration into your own personal amusement, you'll see just how entertaining it can be!

Do you have favorite meanings and interpretations of political talk that you want to share?

Use the following pages to jot down your favorites and come to our website to post them. Check out our latest books while you're there.

www.dontmisunderstandme.com

Thank you –
Merrilee & Jason

My Favorite Meanings of Every Day Political Conversation: NOTES

1. Phrase: _____

_____

Meanings: _____

_____

_____

2. Phrase: _____

_____

Meanings: _____

_____

_____

3. Phrase: _____

_____

Meanings: _____

_____

_____

4. Phrase: _____

_____

Meanings: _____

_____

_____

5. Phrase: _____

_____

Meanings: _____

_____

_____

6. Phrase: _____

_____

Meanings: _____

_____

_____

www.ingramcontent.com/pod-product-compliance
Lightning Source LLC
Chambersburg PA
CBHW021005090426
42738CB00007B/664